# THE RIGHT
# TO PRIVACY

The Right to Privacy (Legal Legends Series), with Foreword

Original work published in 1890 by Samuel D. Warren and Louis D. Brandeis, in Volume 4 of Harvard Law Review. No copyright is claimed in the original text; in any quoted statutes, regulations, or excerpts from court opinions; or in accompublic domain photography and clippings.

Printed in the United States of America.

ISBN: 1452819246

ISBN EAN-13: 9781452819242

Category: Law/Privacy

**qp**

**Quid Pro Law Books**

Quid Pro, LLC

5860 Citrus Blvd., Suite D-101

New Orleans, Louisiana 70123

*quidprolaw@gmail.com*

# THE RIGHT
# TO PRIVACY

Samuel D. Warren

and

Louis D. Brandeis

*with a 2010 Foreword*

*by Steven Alan Childress*

Legal Legends Series

**qp**

**Quid Pro Law Books**

# TABLE OF CONTENTS

# FOREWORD

When Boston law partners Samuel Warren and Louis Brandeis penned the 1890 article "The Right to Privacy," they changed the world. Seldom is that feat accomplished by stuffy works of legal academe published in the tony journals of U.S. law schools, even the *Harvard Law Review.* Most law review articles are hardly read, much less effective and influential. But this one was not stuffy – it was elegant and painstaking, clever and readable. And it hooked into an emotional sense of privacy that resonated with readers and lawmakers for decades, and still hits home today.

This article was more than just influential. It has become, starting out of the gates and throughout a dozen decades of legal change, one of the most- cited law review articles in history – and very likely the most important, game-changing piece of legal scholarship ever. It invented a whole field of law. Later its spillover repercussions, some unwittingly perhaps, were felt in more current debates over informational privacy, abortion, contraception, the "right to die," government surveillance, medical disclosures, drug testing, and sexual orientation. Beyond tort law, as simply put by Judge Richard Posner in a 1995 opinion, "the legal concept of privacy . . . originated in a famous article by Warren and Brandeis."[1] When you see pro-life activists

---

[1] Anderson v. Romero, 72 F.3d 518, 521 (7th Cir. 1995). Even critics agree that it is "the most influential law review article of all." Harry Kalven, Jr., *Privacy in Tort Law – Were Warren and Brandeis Wrong?*, 31 Law & Contemp. Probs. 326, 327 (1966) . Of course, if Brandeis were a law professor today, he would have to overcome,

picketing clinics and the U.S. Supreme Court, you can trace their outrage back to the recognition that privacy matters and is a legal right.

Warren and Brandeis undoubtedly did not intend all these currents downstream from the ripple they instigated, and some of the argument's logical implications have proved troublesome in light of the First Amendment free-speech positions that Brandeis famously took when he became a [great] Justice of the U.S. Supreme Court. Nevertheless, the power they unleashed went beyond the common law argument they fashioned.

The article and its affirmative sense that the law must protect individuals in their multiple spheres of private life remain poignant in modern times and in a variety of legal contexts. It has even influenced the *constitutional* law applied in U.S. courts today, although the article was never about constitutional limits on privacy as such. Yet just in its more modest realm of the common law (well, modest on hindsight, as it may have been quite radical at the time), in recognizing within the law of states a civil and non-contractual right of protection against invasions of privacy, the article was nothing short of momentous.

It also is a good read, for lawyer and nonlawyer alike. These two knew how to write, and they picked a subject people care deeply about. There is every historical

---

with his tenure committee, the problem that the article was *co*-written and published while he was a practitioner. Plus it was useful. But he might be aided by the possibility that the work had less usefulness in England, as recently asserted by Neil Richards & Daniel Solove, *Privacy's Other Path: Recovering the Law of Confidentiality*, 96 Geo. L.J. 123 (2007-2008).

evidence that they cared deeply about it, too, in ways they do not let on in the article itself. They had something of an agenda at work here, and the backstory is interesting. But even standing on its own – and not simply as a polemical reflex from a Warren personally touched by a nosey press, or a young Brandeis's opening salvo in what would become a rock star life in the law – it is a fascinating read that stands the test of time. Plus it foreshadowed big chunks of that time.

Even pop culture may owe some debt to this article. It has to be the most important byproduct in human history of a possible *paparazzi* incident (more on this later), and could have taught Sean Penn a lesson or two. Moreover, we may not have a cult of personality today, or talk so openly about individuality and privacy beyond law, had these two men not put their finger on, and articulated, the concept of an "inviolate personality." Their evocative prose touches on many themes in law and culture, and even seems inadvertently to use emoticons. That's a stretch, to be sure, but they did allude to the theft of that personality as "piracy" and denied this was about "judicial legislation" (because of the law's "elasticity") in a way that some would recognize as not only modern, but *postmodern.*

Another very modern theme of this article is its emphasis on emerging technology as a threat to personal privacy as well as a reason, in turn, to develop the law:  indeed, they say (at note 40) that law's "greatest boast" is "its adaptability to new conditions, the capacity for growth," which reacts to "an ever changing society" to meet its needs.  Their era's tech may seem quaint today – they fret about cameras that do not require the subject to sit for minutes (so allowing surreptitious photography)[2] and the expansion of the print media (so allowing widespread distribution of secrets). But the idea that this makes a difference in what the rule of law should *be* seems fresh today, even as the particular technologies have changed and have, some would say, multiplied these concerns geometrically. Yet just in pushing a theme that technology means change and change means legal reform, this article is a crucial advancement in legal thought. Their argument gave specific attention to one fast-changing example of what Oliver Wendell Holmes, Jr. had previously called the law's need to respond to the "felt necessities of the time."[3]

Moreover, the article's influence has extended beyond substantive tort law, even past the far broader notions of privacy enforced by courts today. Apart from its take on the specific subject, it appears to be, less famously, a pioneering and educational model of what a great legal article or book should be.[4] It has influenced generations of law professors, practitioners, and judges in how to write about law and to fashion a persuasive argument – in articles, briefs, and judicial opinions having nothing whatsoever to do with privacy or individualism. Warren and Brandeis demonstrated, in

---

[2] Also, truly *amateur* photography, without a contract as Warren and Brandeis discuss, had become the craze by 1890, notably with the sale of George Eastman's new "Kodak" camera.

[3] Oliver W. Holmes, Jr., The Common Law 1 (1881). Holmes' classic work is also part of the Legal Legend Series (Quid Pro Law, fthcg. 2010).

[4] Almost immediately it was recognized as "one of the most brilliant excursions in the field of theoretical jurisprudence," Elbridge L. Adams, *The Right of Privacy, and its Relation to the Law of Libel*, 39 Am. L. Rev. 37, 37 (1905). It remains so today.

effect, the consummate advocate's brief about law reform, and the model is no doubt used by many today to change law without even realizing that heritage.

Brandeis himself later became famous for the "Brandeis Brief" filed in actual court cases, and that term refers to a more systematic use of nonlegal, factual, and expert sources to drive home a point of law (as he used successfully in 1908, in arguing for employment protection laws). Nonetheless, it is not a big leap to see this article as the first Brandeis Brief of sorts, targeting not a specific court in a real case, but all courts in all such cases. The authors offered a sweeping change in the law while presenting it, perfectly, as the inevitable outgrowth of existing strands of doctrine. It was far more than that.

So why did they care so much about privacy and about (they probably admitted to themselves) the lack of explicit recognition of such a right in common law precedent? For Warren, the impetus was personal, or at least so the story goes; for Brandeis, there may have been an ambition and restlessness of his powerful mind – he had not much earlier graduated from Harvard Law at age 20, sporting its highest average ever – that saw his friend's plight and gave detail to it, and found a way to make a difference beyond his law office work.

Samuel Warren's backstory is legendary, though like many such legends it has become increasingly clear that layers of tradition and legal storytelling turned it into more myth than reality. He was incensed when a yellow-journalism photographer invaded his daughter's wedding and printed photos of discrete moments. As an established lawyer in Boston's elite bar, and a member of a recognized family, Warren did not need that invasion or publicity. He was personally repulsed by the press's conduct and attention to him.

Or at least that is, roughly and simplistically perhaps, how the story goes. Furthermore, the legend had the backing of none other than the later "Dean of Torts," William Prosser (a real dean, famously, at Berkeley from 1948-1961). Prosser eventually shaped and cajoled the new tort of privacy into four categories of accepted law[5] – appropriation of name or likeness, intrusion upon seclusion, false light, and publicizing private facts – all while spinning the yarn about the Boston press versus the blue-blood Warrens and their daughter's wedding.

Turns out, it could not have happened that way. Warren's oldest daughter (of his eventual six children) was, at most, seven years old at the time. She hardly went crying to daddy about those mean *paparazzi* ruining her big day.

The myth was thoroughly debunked in 2008 in a fascinating essay by Professor Amy Gajda.[6] Gajda, then

---

[5] *See* William L. Prosser, *Privacy*, 48 Calif. L. Rev. 383 (1960). Implementation of the four privacy torts was effectively a coup on his part. He wrote the famous article, finding in Warren and Brandeis's work the emergence of four distinct privacy interests. Then as Reporter for the American Law Institute's project on the Restatement of the Law, he set forth these four torts. Then as author of the leading hornbook, *The Law of Torts*, Prosser cited the Restatement for its recognition of four privacy torts. Circular, but effective: state courts quickly recognized the four torts of privacy, even in the *civil* law jurisdiction of Louisiana.

[6] Amy Gajda, *What If Samuel D. Warren Hadn't Married a Senator's Daughter?: Uncovering the Press Coverage That Led to "The Right to Privacy"*, 2008 Mich. St. L. Rev. 35. Other scholars had noted the temporal problem in the face of the "canon" (or just stated their

a professor of journalism and law at the University of Illinois (now joining us on the law faculty of Tulane), scoured more than sixty newspaper clippings of the day to put to rest the Prosser-fueled myth of the daughter's nuptials and even other, more plausible accounts.

Out of this research is born, or at least suggested, a new legend: Warren married a U.S. Senator's daughter and thereby fell into the world of "gossip-mongers" and sensational journalism, a "social blight" that follows only those in the public eye. He seemed to be an unwilling conscript to this attention, and reacted negatively to newspaper reports and photos of his own wedding – wedding crashers, to him, were apparently not welcome at the Senator's daughter's ceremony and two after-parties.

It was, wrote *The Washington Post*, the "marriage of the season." But what about that successful lawyer Samuel Warren? "There was a bridegroom, too, but bridegrooms are seldom much noticed on occasions of this kind, and he may be passed by with this remark, that there was a bridegroom."[7] Ouch.[8] At least he may have achieved, with the aid of the even-less-mentioned

---

perplexed nature at Warren's motivation), but Gajda's effort is the most sustained and snopes-esque. Before, it was increasingly perceived that Warren's own appearances in the Boston press were surprisingly few (in light of the myth, at least), and fairly benign.

Some of the photos and clippings relevant to this article are included in this work, and were generously provided by Prof. Gajda from her research. The editor thanks her for allowing their inclusion in the book.

[7] *See* Gajda, 2008 Mich. St. L. Rev. at 36-37.

[8] True, but ouch. Facts though entirely true may really harm, as the article ironically makes clear in distinguishing the common law of libel for false facts that affect reputation.

Brandeis, some measure of revenge on the *Post* (something Richard Nixon could hardly claim).[9] It also may not have helped matters that the press had a field day reporting, a year before the article was published, all over his father-in-law's marriage to a woman twenty years younger than the groom[10] (and not much older than Mrs. Warren). This attention, and speculation about the relationship between the Senator's daughters and their new stepmom, may have prompted Warren to write this, though ironically his plea for privacy made him . . . famous.

"It is probably no coincidence," Gajda writes, "that much of the coverage" of the Warren family over the years "is contained in articles headlined with the word 'gossip.' "[11] Fourteen, in fact. The word, and variations on the theme, appear throughout the 1890 article: gossip has become a "trade" which "attains the dignity of print," these legal legends lamented.

That lament, from whatever motivations the two shared, spawned the most significant law review project ever.

-- *Steven Alan Childress*

---

[9] Though interestingly, the attorney later arguing in the Supreme Court for the right to privacy in the face of a new constitutional defense asserted by the press? None other than private citizen Richard Nixon, in losing his clients' claim under a privacy tort. *See* Time, Inc. v. Hill, 385 U.S. 374 (1967). He often expressed outrage about press invasion of private people, like his clients, in statements echoing the Warren meme. Nixon was also present in Dallas the day Kennedy was killed, for a meeting with Pepsi executives. Small world.

[10] *See* Gajda, 2008 Mich. St. L. Rev. at 41-42.

[11] *Id.* at 44.

# Biography

***Samuel Dennis Warren*** was born in Dedham, Massachusetts, in 1852, the son of wealthy and prominent New England parents. He attended Harvard Law School and graduated in 1877 second to only one other student – Brandeis. They eventually formed a law firm and practiced law in Boston. Warren's marriage to Mabel Bayard, daughter of a Senator (and presidential candidate, Secretary of State, and ambassador to Great Britain), began in 1883.

Before Warren published "The Right to Privacy" in 1890, he coauthored two other articles with Brandeis in the new *Harvard Law Review*. By the time of their famous article, Warren had actually withdrawn from their law partnership to run his recently deceased father's paper company. Warren himself died in 1910 at the age of 57. His obituary, reproduced at page xxiii, was ironically spare in light of the reporting before which had caused him to make a federal case out of it.

***Louis Dembitz Brandeis***, born in 1856 in Louisville, Kentucky to Jewish immigrants, became one the most important legal figures in American history. Brandeis attended Harvard Law School and graduated in 1877, briefly practicing law in St. Louis before returning to Boston to work with Warren. Brandeis married in 1891, the year after "The Right to Privacy" was published, and eventually he and Alice Goldmark Brandeis had two children. In addition to his influential writings and advocacy for liberal causes exemplified by the "Brandeis Brief," and earning him the nickname "the people's attorney," in 1914 he wrote the nicely titled book *Other People's Money, and How The Bankers Use It,* opposing large banks, monopolies, and corporate power.

Over the years, he became a frequent supporter of educational, Zionist, and political causes (many of which he secretly continued, questionably under current concepts of judicial ethics, long after he joined the Supreme Court).[12]

Brandeis became an Associate Justice of the U.S. Supreme Court in 1916. Appointed by Woodrow Wilson, he was not easily confirmed, as the first Jewish member of the Court (and as a "radical," averred former President William H. Taft, later his colleague on the bench). Brandeis served there until 1939. He died in 1941 at age 84.

On the Court, he became known for his dissents and concurrences, and his magnificent dissenting opinions outlived their immediate effect of falling on the losing side of a case. They withstood the judgment of history, and many became the Court's accepted rule years later. While many of them showed deference to legislative power and reluctance to a constitutional judicial activism, his opinions promoting the free speech right influenced constitutional doctrine for generations,

---

[12] The little-discussed reality of his continuing political activism and private consulting to politicians and causes, in ways that would not be acceptable today (and probably were not then, had they been known), are well documented in the excellent book by Bruce Allen Murphy, The Brandeis/Frankfurter Connection (1982). Justice Felix Frankfurter, appointed in 1939 as Brandeis was retiring, continued this tradition even while proclaiming publicly that "this Court has no excuse for being unless it's a monastery." *Id.* at 9. His official position was that he was a "political eunuch." The truth for both Justices was far more complicated, as Murphy debunks some of the myths surrounding these legal giants.

particularly his powerful concurrence, as joined by Holmes, in *Whitney v. California*, 274 U.S. 357 (1927). On civil procedure and federalism, he penned the landmark decision in *Erie Railroad Co. v. Tompkins*, 304 U.S. 64 (1938), ending the reign of federal common law.

Notably, too, Brandeis wrote about freedom from government intrusion into privacy, in a wiretapping case. Dissenting in *Olmstead v. United States*, 277 U.S. 438 (1928), against the majority opinion by Chief Justice Taft, Brandeis found in the U.S. Constitution the Framers' intention for people to have "the right to be let alone – the most comprehensive of rights and the right most valued by civilized men." Some of the same language, and much of the sentiment, is found in his 1890 article, though this time it was in service of a constitutional right. (The Supreme Court overturned the *Olmstead* rule in 1967, in yet another posthumous victory for Brandeis.)

Some of Brandeis's developing First Amendment views may not be, upon reflection, entirely consistent with the governmental power against the press that would follow from recognizing the privacy tort he envisioned – though perhaps you will find reconciliation in the article's final section on the limits of the new right to privacy and its test for matters in the public interest. In any event, the inherent tension between a free citizenry and press, and the asserted right to be left alone,[13] is but one of the sub-stories and after-effects of his landmark article that make it so intriguing.

---

[13]    In a forthcoming 2010 article, Neal Richards, a law professor at Washington University, explores this famous tension and offers his own reconciliation, arguing that Brandeis's view of privacy morphed over the years (as enabling an active citizenry) to become

## *What to look for in this edition of*

## *"The Right to Privacy"*

I have tried as much as possible to recreate the article exactly as Warren and Brandeis published it in the nascent *Harvard Law Review*. My effort turned out to be surprisingly rare because the online and digital versions I compared to the original source article all failed to produce it accurately. Several even edited their own words into the material without indicating so. Needless to say, they did not improve it. I determined to let the words live without channeling through me; the reader deserves that respect, as do these giants of legal thought.

Because this edition was also produced for digital books with their fluid locations and linkable footnotes, there are some formatting realities that must appear consistently in each version (and make the print version flow better as well, fortunately). To that end, there are a few alterations on both versions that I hope you will find acceptable; I thought they were essential to the format, while still meeting my goal of rendering their work as accurately as feasible.

- I re-inserted the original page numbers into the text, so readers can cite the article correctly or reference passages in it to others. They appear in {brackets}.

---

consistent with his championing of free speech rights. It is a very good article to read (available so far only on SSRN) both to learn about the usual view of this tension and his own response to it.

- The footnotes are numbered sequentially from 1 to 53. In the original, footnotes re-started at 1 on each new page. Digital books typically use mutable locations rather than fixed pages (to accommodate font sizing and text to speech), so that was out. Even with a version with pages, the reader would get lost in the recycling footnote numbers – there would be some 25 footnote 1's. My new footnote numbers do match most every online source and seem to be an accepted format for this work. For legal citation purposes, the original footnote number may be readily deduced in either version, using the {page breaks} noted.

- The footnotes in the print version remained as footnotes, but digitally are now endnotes, as they must be in an ebook that is not fixed. (But I have made sure that the notes in that version are linked, to jump back and forth easily.) At any rate, the beauty of this work, in my opinion, is in the text and not the intricate and legalistic (but necessary for its purposes) notes. Reading only the text makes complete sense—another lesson to be learned from this model of legal writing. Please trust me that the textual points are amply supported in detailed precedent and other sources. (Having said that, check out the eloquent discourse on judicial activism and law's "elasticity" hidden in note 40: we are not urging "judicial legislation"! And I marvel at the several later citations to French sources.)

- I have made minor, consistent spacing changes throughout for legibility and flow without changing the words or quotability in any way.

- I have added a solid line between sections to show where the authors divided the article using extra line spacing. It is clear that they presented the material in separate parts, and I have added a Table of Contents to reflect that.

- I used the arabic numeral 1 where the authors intended that, unlike most sources that present this as a roman I. You should know that the *Harvard Law Review*, like *Reader's Digest*, thinks that the *Titanic* sank in 1912. On April 14.

This edition was designed primarily for a digital platform, where the gap in accuracy and need for working footnotes is greatest. That work is available as identification number B003HS5NM2 and can be read not only on the Kindle, but also using free ereader applications on such devices as Windows PC, Mac, BlackBerry, iPhone, iTouch, and iPad.

-- S.A.C.

## About this edition and its editor

The *Legal Legends Series* offers high quality digital renditions of classic legal scholarship, adding active tables of contents and linked footnotes while minimizing the formatting and scanning errors common in such works. Each book is painstakingly checked against original sources and is not derivative of online versions. All books in the Series imbed the original page numbers for easy citation. In addition, new Forewords by contemporary legal scholars place the works in historical context and provide biographical background on the lives and influences of the authors.

Accompanying print versions are available, such as this edition.

The publisher welcomes comments, questions, and formatting suggestions, as well as suggestions for new additions to the Series with original and descriptive Forewords. Contemporary, original material may be submitted as well.

*Steven Alan Childress* is the Conrad Meyer III Professor of Law at Tulane University, where he teaches legal ethics, torts, and evidence. Alan earned his law degree from Harvard and a Ph.D. in Jurisprudence and Social Policy from Berkeley, as well as a B.A. from Alabama. He writes about ethics, federal courts, and the First Amendment. He co-authored *Federal Standards of Review*. Its fourth edition, published by LexisNexis in three volumes, is available in 2010; previous editions have been cited by law professors and over 300 courts, including the Supreme Court. He co-edits *The Legal Profession Blog*. Alan is a member of the California, District of Columbia, and Supreme Court bars, Phi Beta Kappa, and the Law & Society Association.

# Photography

and

# news clippings

from the *New York Times*

Louis D. Brandeis

Brandeis, likely in his law office

The younger Brandeis

# THE WASHINGTON SOCIETY WORLD.

## MARRIAGE OF SENATOR BAYARD'S DAUGHTER
### —A RECEPTION AND TWO BANQUETS.

WASHINGTON, Jan. 25.—The wedding of Miss Mabel Bayard, eldest daughter of Senator Bayard, of Delaware, and Mr. Samuel D. Warren, Jr., of Boston, took place at the Church of the Ascension this morning in the presence of a distinguished company of invited guests. The ceremony was performed by the Rev. Dr. Elliot. There were 10 ushers and 8 brides-maids. The bride, leaning upon the arm of her father, entered the church at 11:45, and was met at the chancel-rail by the groom and his best man, Mr. Wetmore, of Michigan. The bride's dress was of heavy white satin, the back of the train falling in long folds and the front covered with point lace flounces. Paniers were shirred across the hips, and the high corsage was cut with square neck and elbow sleeves and finished with point lace. Her only ornaments were a string of gold beads around her throat. Her bouquet was of white roses, and the long tulle veil was confined to the head by a chaplet of orange blossoms. The eight brides-maids were the two Misses Bayard, sisters of the bride, Miss Warren, Miss Crebbs, Miss Marshall, Miss Andrews, Miss Kane, and Miss Lockwood. The dresses of these bride's attendants were of white mull, over silk, the skirts demi-train, and the fronts covered with ruffles of pompadour and Aurillac lace. They wore large white Gainsborough hats, covered with white plumes and faced with sapphire and ruby velvet, each bridesmaid carrying a bouquet of colored roses in her hand.

The reception that followed at the residence of Senator Bayard was a large affair, and the house was crowded until the bride and groom departed to take the 4 o'clock train for the North. An elaborate collation was served in the dining-room, and souvenirs of wedding cake were provided for the guests. Many handsome presents were made, but were not displayed. Among those present were the Russian, Danish, Argentine, Portuguese, and Spanish Ministers and their families; Senator and Mrs. Cameron, Senator Jones, Senator and Mrs. Pendleton, W. W. Story and wife, Mr. Morrill, and Miss Swan, Miss Frelinghuysen, Mrs. Brewster, Mme. Catalano, Mrs. Stephen Field, Mrs. John Davis, Mrs. George B. Loring, Gen. and Miss Schenck, Mr. and Miss Yulee, the Rev. Dorus Clark, and Mr. and Mrs. Warren. Senator Bayard gave a dinner of 14 covers at Wormley's this evening to the party of Boston friends who came here to be present at his daughter's wedding.

Senator Hoar gave a dinner at Wormley's this evening. Covers were laid for 32 persons, and the board was profusely decorated with flowers. A border of flowers surrounded the table and three large oval baskets of flowers were placed in the centre. A ball of flowers hung from the ceiling over the middle of the table. The host sat at the centre of the table, with Mr. E. B. Haskell, of Boston, on his right and Mr. Green on his left. The other guests were the Hon. George Bancroft, ex-Gov. Rice, Senators Dawes, Hawley, Anthony, Morrill, and Hale, Representatives Rice, Crapo, Bowman, Candler, Morse, Ranney, Robinson, Stone, Norcross, Russell, Harris, and Singleton, Commissioner Loring, the Hon. John B. Alley, Major Poor, and Messrs. Hudson, Wright, Barrett, Gilson, McFarland, Parker, and Stetson.

# RICH MEN'S CONDUCTOR DEAD.

### Engineer of "Millionaires' Express," Taken Ill Same Day, near Death.

David Sanderson, conductor of "the Millionaire Express," running between Morristown, N. J., and Hoboken for the last twenty-five years, died yesterday at his Morristown home after an illness of two weeks. Engineer Benjamin Day of the same train is lying desperately ill in the railroad's hospital at Scranton, Penn., where it is said his chances for recovery are small.

Both Engineer Day and Conductor Sanderson finished their morning run from Morristown to Hoboken two weeks ago, and reported sick. Sanderson requested that he be allowed to go to his home, and Day asked that he be sent to the company's Scranton hospital.

Sanderson had been in the railroad business all his life, and conductor of "the Millionaire Express" since the inauguration of the train twenty-five years ago. He was 67 years old at the time of his death, and was known to every commuter between Morristown and Hoboken. He is survived by a wife and two children.

## Samuel D. Warren Dead.

BOSTON, Feb. 20.—Samuel Dennis Warren died of apoplexy to-day at his home in Dedham. Mr. Warren was the son of Samuel Dennis Warren, and was born in 1852. He was graduated from Harvard in 1875 and from the law school in 1877. For a time he was in partnership with Louis D. Brandeis, now counsel for L. R. Glavis, at Washington. In 1899 he relinquished the law and became a paper manufacturer, with mills in Maine. His wife was Miss Mabel Bayard, daughter of Thomas F. Bayard, whom he married at Washington in 1883. She survives him with six children.

## Dr. Monroe Budd Long.

Dr. Monroe Budd Long, one of the best-known physicians in New Jersey, died yesterday at his home, 546 Park Avenue, Plainfield, N. J. Dr. Long was born in Martinsville, N. J., in 1849. He was graduated from the College of Physicians and Surgeons in this city in 1874. The next year he settled in Plainfield, and later became associated with Dr. Joel Suthen. He succeeded to the practice when Dr. Suthen died in 1885. Dr. Long leaves a widow, three daughters, and two sons. Mrs. Long before her marriage in 1877 was Miss Cora Goodman of Newark.

## J. S. Cram's Mother Dies; He Is Away.

Mrs. Katherine Sergeant Cram, widow of the late Henry A. Cram, the lawyer, and mother of J. Sergeant Cram, died on Saturday at her home, 5 East Thirty-eighth Street, in her 87th year. She had been ill about two weeks. Her daughter, Miss Lillian Cram, and her granddaughter, Miss Charlotte Cram, lived with her. She also leaves another daughter, Mrs. J. Woodward Haven of 18 East Seventy-ninth Street. J. Sergeant Cram is in South Carolina on a hunting trip as the guest of R. T. Wilson. Messengers have been sent into the woods to notify him of his mother's death.

Obit

# THE RIGHT TO PRIVACY

---

Samuel D. Warren

and

Louis D. Brandeis

*Harvard Law Review*

Vol. IV     December 15, 1890     No. 5

# THE RIGHT TO PRIVACY.

"It could be done only on principles of private justice, moral fitness, and public convenience, which, when applied to a new subject, make common law without a precedent; much more when received and approved by usage."

WILLES, J., in Millar *v.* Taylor, 4 Burr. 2303, 2312.

THAT the individual shall have full protection in person and in property is a principle as old as the common law; but it has been found necessary from time to time to define anew the exact nature and extent of such protection. Political, social, and economic changes entail the recognition of new rights, and the common law, in its eternal youth, grows to meet the new demands of society. Thus, in very early times, the law gave a remedy only for physical interference with life and property, for trespasses *vi et armis*. Then the "right to life" served only to protect the subject from battery in its various forms; liberty meant freedom from actual restraint; and the right to property secured to the individual his lands and his cattle. Later, there came a recognition of man's spiritual nature, of his feelings and his intellect. Gradually the scope of these legal rights broadened; and now the right to life has come to mean the right to enjoy life, — the right to be let alone; the right to liberty secures the exercise of extensive civil privileges; and the term "property" has grown to comprise every form of possession — intangible, as well as tangible.

Thus, with the recognition of the legal value of sensations, the protection against actual bodily injury was extended to prohibit mere attempts to do such injury; that is, the putting another in {194} fear of such injury. From the action of battery grew that of assault.[1] Much later there came a qualified protection of the

---

[1] Year Book, Lib. Ass., folio 99, pl. 60 (1348 or 1349), appears to be the first reported case where damages were recovered for a civil assault.

individual against offensive noises and odors, against dust and smoke, and excessive vibration. The law of nuisance was developed.[2] So regard for human emotions soon extended the scope of personal immunity beyond the body of the individual. His reputation, the standing among his fellow-men, was considered, and the law of slander and libel arose.[3] Man's family relations became a part of the legal conception of his life, and the alienation of a wife's affections was held remediable. [4] Occasionally the law halted, as in its refusal to recognize the intrusion by seduction upon the honor of the family. But even here the demands of society were met. A mean fiction, the action *per quod servitium amisit*, was resorted to, and by allowing damages for injury to the parents' feelings, an adequate remedy was ordinarily afforded.[5]

---

[2] These nuisances are technically injuries to property; but the recognition of the right to have property free from interference by such nuisances involves also a recognition of the value of human sensations.

[3] Year Book, Lib. Ass., folio 177, pl. 19 (1356), (2 Finl. Reeves Eng. Law, 395) seems to be the earliest reported case of an action for slander.

[4] Winsmore *v.* Greenbank, Willes, 577 (1745).

[5] Loss of service is the gist of the action; but it has been said that "we are not aware of any reported case

Similar to the expansion of the right to life was the growth of the legal conception of property. From corporeal property arose the incorporeal rights issuing out of it; and then there opened the wide realm of intangible property, in the products and processes of the mind,[6] **{195}** as

---

brought by a parent where the value of such services was held to be the measure of damages." Cassoday, K., in Lavery *v.* Crooke, 52 Wis. 612, 623 (1881). First the fiction of constructive service was invented; Martin *v.* Paine, 9 John. 387 (1812). Then the feelings of the parent, the dishonor to himself and his family, were accepted as the most important element of damage. Bedford *v.* McKowl, 3 Esp. 1992 (1800); Andrews *v.* Askey, 8 C. & P. 7 (1837); Philips *v.* Hoyle, 4 Gray, 568 (1855); Phelin *v.* Kenderline, 20 Pa. St. 354 (1853). The allowance of these damages would seem to be a recognition that the invasion upon the honor of the family is an injury to the parent's person, for ordinarily mere injury to parental feelings is not an element of damage, *e.g,* the suffering of the parent in case of physical injury to the child. Flemington *v.* Smithers, 2 C. & P. 292 (1827); Black *v.* Carrolton R. R. Co., 10 La. Ann. 33 (1855); Covington Street Ry. Co. *v.* Packer, 9 Bush, 455 (1872).

6 "The notion of Mr. Justice Yates that nothing is property which cannot be earmarked and recovered in detinue or trover, may be true in an early stage of society, when property is in its simple form, and the remedies for violation of it also simple, but is not true in a more civilized state, when the relations of life and the interests arising therefrom are complicated." Erle, J., in Jefferys *v.* Boosey, 4 H. L. C. 815, 869 (1854).

4

works of literature and art,[7]goodwill,[8] trade secrets, and trademarks.[9]

This development of the law was inevitable. The intense intellectual and emotional life, and the heightening of sensations which came with the advance of civilization, made it clear to men that only a part of the pain, pleasure, and profit of life lay in physical things. Thoughts, emotions, and sensations demanded legal recognition, and the beautiful capacity for growth which characterizes the common law enabled the judges to afford the requisite protection, without the interposition of the legislature.

Recent inventions and business methods call attention to the next step which must be taken for the protection of the person, and for securing to the individual what Judge Cooley

---

[7] Copyright appears to have been first recognized as a species of private property in England in 1558. Drone on Copyright, 54, 61.

[8] Gibblett v. Read, 9 Mod. 459 (1743), is probably the first recognition of goodwill as property.

[9] Hogg v. Kirby, 8 Ves. 215 (1803). As late as 1742 Lord Hardwicke refused to treat a trade-mark as property for infringement upon which an injunction could be granted. Blanchard v. Hill, 2 Atk. 484.

calls the right "to be let alone."[10] Instantaneous photographs and newspaper enterprise have invaded the sacred precincts of private and domestic life; and numerous mechanical devices threaten to make good the prediction that "what is whispered in the closet shall be proclaimed from the house-tops." For years there has been a feeling that the law must afford some remedy for the unauthorized circulation of portraits of private persons;[11] and the evil of invasion of privacy by the newspapers, long keenly felt, has been but recently discussed by an able writer.[12] The alleged facts of a somewhat notorious case brought before an inferior tribunal in New York a few months ago,[13] directly involved the consideration {196}

---

[10] Cooley on Torts, 2d ed., p. 29.

[11] 8 Amer. Law Reg. N. S. 1 (1869); 12 Wash. Law Rep. 353 (1884); 24 Sol. J. & Rep. 4 (1879).

[12] Scribner's Magazine, July, 1890. "The Rights of the Citizen: To his Reputation," by E.L. Godkin, Esq., pp. 65, 67.

[13] Marion Manola v. Stevens & Myers, N.Y. Supreme Court, "New York Times" of June 15, 18, 21, 1890. There the complainant alleged that while she was playing in the Broadway Theatre, in a role which required her appearance in tights, she was, by means of a flash light, photographed surreptitiously and without her consent, from one of the boxes by defendant Stevens, the manager of the "Castle in the Air" company,

of the right of circulating portraits; and the question whether our law will recognize and protect the right to privacy in this and in other respects must soon come before our courts for consideration.

Of the desirability — indeed of the necessity — of some such protection, there can, it is believed, be no doubt. The press is overstepping in every direction the obvious bounds of propriety and of decency. Gossip is no longer the resource of the idle and of the vicious, but has become a trade, which is pursued with industry as well as effrontery. To satisfy a prurient taste the details of sexual relations are spread broadcast in the columns of the daily papers. To occupy the indolent, column upon column is filled with idle gossip, which can only be procured by intrusion upon the domestic circle. The intensity and complexity of life, attendant upon advancing civilization, have rendered necessary some retreat from the world, and man, under the refining influence of culture, has become more

---

and defendant Myers, a photographer, and prayed that the defendants might be restrained from making use of the photograph taken. A preliminary injunction issued *ex parte*, and a time was set for argument of the motion that the injunction should be made permanent, but no one then appeared in opposition.

sensitive to publicity, so that solitude and privacy have become more essential to the individual; but modern enterprise and invention have, through invasions upon his privacy, subjected him to mental pain and distress, far greater than could be inflicted by mere bodily injury. Nor is the harm wrought by such invasions confined to the suffering of those who may be the subjects of journalistic or other enterprise. In this, as in other branches of commerce, the supply creates the demand. Each crop of unseemly gossip, thus harvested, becomes the seed of more, and, in direct proportion to its circulation, results in the lowering of social standards and of morality. Even gossip apparently harmless, when widely and persistently circulated, is potent for evil. It both belittles and perverts. It belittles by inverting the relative importance of things, thus dwarfing the thoughts and aspirations of a people. When personal gossip attains the dignity of print, and crowds the space available for matters of real interest to the community, what wonder that the ignorant and thoughtless mistake its relative importance. Easy of comprehension, appealing to that weak side of human nature which is never wholly cast down by the misfortunes and frailties of our neighbors, no one can be surprised that it usurps the place of interest in brains capable of other things. Triviality destroys at once robustness of thought and delicacy of feeling. No enthusiasm can flourish, no generous impulse can survive under its blighting influence. {197}

It is our purpose to consider whether the existing law affords a principle which can properly be invoked to protect the privacy of the individual; and, if it does, what the nature and extent of such protection is.

---

Owing to the nature of the instruments by which privacy is invaded, the injury inflicted bears a superficial resemblance to the wrongs dealt with by the law of slander and of libel, while a legal remedy for such injury seems to involve the treatment of mere wounded feelings, as a substantive cause of action. The principle on which the law of defamation rests, covers, however, a radically different class of effects from those for which attention is now asked. It deals only with damage to reputation, with the injury done to the individual in his external relations to the community, by lowering him in the estimation of his fellows. The matter published of him, however widely circulated, and however unsuited to publicity, must, in order to be actionable, have a direct tendency to injure him in his intercourse with others, and even if in writing or in print, must subject him to the hatred, ridicule, or contempt of his fellow-men,—the effect of the publication upon his estimate of himself and upon his own feelings nor forming an essential element in the cause of action.   In short, the wrongs and correlative rights recognized by the law of slander and libel are in their nature material rather than spiritual.   That branch of the law simply extends the protection surrounding physical property to certain of the conditions necessary or helpful to worldly prosperity.   On the other hand, our law recognizes no principle upon which compensation can be granted for mere injury to the feelings.   However painful the mental effects upon another of an act, though purely wanton or even malicious, yet if the act itself is otherwise lawful, the suffering inflicted is *damnum absque injuria*.   Injury of feelings may indeed be taken account of in ascertaining the amount of damages when attending what is recognized as a legal injury;[14]

---

[14] Though the legal value of "feelings" is now generally recognized, distinctions have been drawn between the several classes of cases in which compensation may or may not be recovered.   Thus, the fright occasioned by an assault constitutes a cause of action, but fright

{198} but our system, unlike the Roman law, does not afford a remedy even for mental suffering which results from mere contumely and insult, but from an intentional and

---

occasioned by negligence does not. So fright coupled with bodily injury cannot be relied upon as an element of damages, even where a valid cause of action exists, as in trespass *quare clausum fregit.* Wyman *v.* Leavitt, 71 Me. 227; Canning *v.* Williamstown, 1 Cush. 451. The allowance of damages for injury to the parents' feelings, in case of seduction, adbuction of a child (Stowe *v.* Heywood, 7 All. 188) or removal of the corpse of child from a burial-ground (Meagher *v.* Driscoll, 99 Mass. 281), are said to be exceptions to a general rule. On the other hand, injury to feelings is a recognized element of damages in actions of slander and libel, and of malicious prosecution. These distinctions between the cases, where injury to feelings does and where it does not constitute a cause of action or legal element of damages, are not logical, but doubtless serve well as practical rules. It will, it is believed, be found, upon examination of the authorities, that wherever substantial mental suffering would be the natural and probable result of the act, there compensation for injury to feelings has been allowed, and that where no mental suffering would ordinarily result, or if resulting, would naturally be but trifling, and, being unaccompanied by visible signs of injury, would afford a wide scope for imaginative ills, there damages have been disallowed. The decisions on this subject illustrate well the subjection in our law of logic to common-sense.

unwarranted violation of the "honor" of another.[15]

It is not however necessary, in order to sustain the view that the common law recognizes and upholds a principle applicable to cases of invasion of privacy, to invoke the analogy, which is but superficial, to injuries sustained, either by an attack upon reputation or by what the civilians called a violation of honor; for the legal doctrines relating to infractions of what is ordinarily termed the common-law right to intellectual and artistic property are, it is believed, but instances and applications of a general right to privacy, which properly understood afford a remedy for the evils under consideration.

The common law secures to each individual the right of determining, ordinarily, to what extent his thoughts, sentiments, and emotions

---

[15] "Injuria, in the narrower sense, is every intentional and illegal violation of honour, *i.e.*, the whole personality of another." "Now an outrage is committed not only when a man shall be struck with the fist, say, or with a club, or even flogged, but also if abusive language has been used to one." Salkowski, Roman Law, p. 668 and p. 669, n. 2.

shall be communicated to others.[16] Under our system of government, he can never be compelled to express them (except when upon the witness stand); and even if he has chosen to give them expression, he generally retains the power to fix the limits of the publicity which shall be given them. The existence of this right does not depend upon the particular {199} method of expression adopted. It is immaterial whether it be by word[17] or by signs,[18] in painting,[19] by sculpture, or in music.[20] Neither does the existence of the right depend upon the nature or value of the thought or emotions, nor upon the excellence of the means of expression.[21] The same protection is accorded

---

[16] "It is certain every man has a right to keep his own sentiments, if he pleases. He has certainly a right to judge whether he will make them public, or commit them only to the sight of his friends." Yates, J., in Millar v. Taylor, 4 Burr. 2303, 2379 (1769).

[17] Nicols v. Pitman, 26 Ch. D. 374 (1884).

[18] Lee v. Simpson, 3 C. B. 871, 881; Daly v. Palmer, 6 Blatchf. 256.

[19] Turner v. Robinson, 10 Ir. Ch. 121; s. c. ib. 510.

[20] Drone on Copyright, 102.

[21] "Assuming the law to be so, what is its foundation in this respect? It is not, I conceive, referable to any consideration peculiarly literary. Those with whom our common law originated has not probably among their

to a casual letter or an entry in a diary and to the most valuable poem or essay, to a botch or daub and to a masterpiece. In every such case the individual is entitled to decide whether that which is his shall be given to the public.[22] No

---

many merits that of being patrons of letters; but they knew the duty and necessity of protecting property, and with that general object laid down rules providently expansive, — rules capable of adapting themselves to the various forms and modes of property which peace and cultivation might discover and introduce.

"The produce of mental labor, thoughts and sentiments, recorded and preserved by writing, became, as knowledge went onward and spread, and the culture of man's understanding advanced, a kind of property impossible to disregard, and the interference of modern legislation upon the subject, by the stat. 8 Anne, professing by its title to be 'For the encouragement of learning" and using the words 'taken the liberty,' in the preamble, whether it operated in augmentation or diminution of the private rights of authors, having left them to some extent untouched, it was found that the common law, in providing for the protection of property, provided for their security, at least before general publication by the writer's consent." Knight Bruce, V.C., in Prince Albert *v.* Strange, 2 DeGex & Sm. 652, 695 (1849).

[22] "The question, however, does not turn upon the form or amount of mischief or advantage, loss or gain. The author of manuscripts, whether he is famous or obscure, low or high, has a right to say of them, if innocent, that whether interesting or dull, light or heavy, saleable or unsaleable, they shall not, without his

other has the right to publish his productions in any form, without his consent. This right is wholly independent of the material on which, the thought, sentiment, or emotions is expressed. It may exist independently of any corporeal being, as in words spoken, a song sung, a drama acted. Or if expressed on any material, as in a poem in writing, the author may have parted with the paper, without forfeiting any proprietary right in the composition itself. The right is lost only when the author himself communicates his production to the public, — in other words, {200} publishes it.[23] It is entirely independent of the copyright laws, and their extension into the domain of art. The aim of those statutes is to secure to the author, composer, or artist the entire profits arising from publication; but the common-law protection enables him to control absolutely the act of publication, and in the exercise of his own discretion, to decide whether there shall be any publication at all.[24] The statutory right is of no value, *unless* there is

---

consent, be published." Knight Bruce, V.C., in Prince Albert *v.* Strange, 2 DeGex & Sm. 652, 694.

[23] Duke of Queensbury *v.* Shebbeare, 2 Eden, 329 (1758); Bartlett *v.* Crittenden, 5 McLean, 32, 41 (1849).

[24] Drone on Copyright, pp. 102, 104; Parton *v.* Prang, 3 Clifford, 537, 548 (1872); Jefferys *v.* Boosey, 4 H. L. C. 815, 867, 962 (1854).

a publication; the common-law right is lost *as soon as* there is a publication.

What is the nature, the basis, of this right to prevent the publication of manuscripts or works of art? It is stated to be the enforcement of a right of property;[25] and no difficulty arises

---

[25] "The question will be whether the bill has stated facts of which the court can take notice, as a case of civil property, which it is bound to protect. The injunction cannot be maintained on any principle of this sort, that if a letter has been written in the way of friendship, either the continuance or the discontinuance of the friendship affords a reason for the interference of the court." Lord Eldon in Gee *v.* Pritchard, 2 Swanst. 402, 413 (1818).

"Upon the principle, therefore, of protecting property, it is that the common law, in cases not aided or prejudiced by statute, shelters the privacy and seclusion of thought and sentiments committed to writing, and desired by the author to remain not generally known." Knight Bruce, V.C., in Prince Albert *v.* Strange, 2 DeGex & Sm. 652, 695.

"It being conceded that reasons of expediency and public policy can never be made the sole basis of civil jurisdiction, the question, whether upon any ground the plaintiff can be entitled to the relief which he claims, remains to be answered; and it appears to us that there is only one ground upon which his title to claim, and our jurisdiction to grant, the relief, can be placed. We must be satisfied, that the publication of private letters, without the consent of the writer, is an

in accepting this view, so long as we have only to deal with the reproduction of literary and artistic compositions. They certainly possess many of the attributes of ordinary property; they are transferable; they have a value; and publication or reproduction is a use by which that value is realized. But where the value of the production is found not in the right to take the profits arising from publication, but in the peace of mind or the relief afforded by the ability to prevent any publication at all, it is difficult to regard the right as one of property, in the common acceptation {201} of that term. A man records in a letter to his son, or in his diary, that he did not dine with his wife on a certain day. No one into whose hands those papers fall could publish them to the world, even if possession of the documents had been obtained rightfully; and the prohibition would not be confined to the publication of a copy of the letter itself, or of the diary entry; the restraint extends also to a publication of the contents. What is the thing which is protected? Surely, not the intellectual act of recording the fact that the husband did not dine with his wife, but that fact itself. It is not the intellectual

---

invasion of an exclusive right of property which remains in the writer, even when the letters have been sent to, and are still in the possession of his correspondent." Duer, J., in Woolsey, v. Judd, 4 Duer, 379, 384 (1855).

product, but the domestic occurrence. A man writes a dozen letters to different people. No person would be permitted to publish a list of the letters written. If the letters or the contents of the diary were protected as literary compositions, the scope of the protection afforded should be the same secured to a published writing under the copyright law. But the copyright law would not prevent an enumeration of the letters, or the publication of some of the facts contained therein. The copyright of a series of paintings or etchings would prevent a reproduction of the paintings as pictures; but it would not prevent a publication of list or even a description of them.[26] Yet in the famous case of {202} Prince

---

[26] "A work lawfully published, in the popular sense of the term, stands in this respect, I conceive, differently from a work which has never been in that situation. The former may be liable to be translated, abridged, analyzed, exhibited in morsels, complimented, and otherwise treated, in a manner that the latter is not.

"Suppose, however, — instead of a translation, an abridgement, or a review, — the case of a catalogue, — suppose a man to have composed a variety of literary works ('innocent,' to use Lord Eldon's expression), which he has never printed or published, or lost the right to prohibit from being published, — suppose a knowledge of them unduly obtained by some unscrupulous person, who prints with a view to circulation a descriptive catalogue, or even a mere list of

Albert *v.* Strange, the court held that the common-law rule prohibited not merely the reproduction of the etchings which the plaintiff and Queen Victoria had made for their own pleasure, but also "the publishing (at least by printing or writing), though not by copy or resemblance, a description of them, whether more or less limited or summary, whether in

---

the manuscripts, without authority or consent, does the law allow this? I hope and believe not. The same principles that prevent more candid piracy must, I conceive, govern such a case also.

"By publishing of a man that he has written to particular persons, or on particular subjects, he may be exposed, not merely to sarcasm, he may be ruined. There may be in his possession returned letters that he had written to former correspondents, with whom to have had relations, however harmlessly, may not in after life be a recommendation; or his wordings may be otherwise of a kind squaring in no sort with his outward habits and worldly position. There are callings even now in which to be convicted of literature, is dangerous, though the danger is sometimes escaped.

"Again, the manuscripts may be those of a man on account of whose name alone a mere list would be matter of general curiosity. How many persons could be mentioned, a catalogue of whose unpublished writings would, during their lives or afterwards, command a ready sale!" Knight Bruce, V.C., in Prince Albert *v.* Strange, 2 DeGex & Sm. 652, 693.

the form of a catalogue or otherwise."[27] Likewise, an unpublished collection of news

[27] "A copy or impression of the etchings would only be a means of communicating knowledge and information of the original, and does not a list and description of the same? The means are different, but the object and effect are similar; for in both, the object and effect is to make known to the public more or less of the unpublished work and composition of the author, which he is entitled to keep wholly for his private use and pleasure, and to withhold altogether, or so far as he may please, from the knowledge of others. Cases upon abridgements, translations, extracts, and criticisms of published works have no reference whatever to the present question; they all depend upon the extent of right under the acts respecting copyright, and have no analogy to the exclusive rights in the author of unpublished compositions which depend entirely upon the common-law right of property." Lord Cottenham in Prince Albert v. Strange, 1 McN. & G 23, 43 (1849). "Mr. Justice Yates, in Millar v. Taylor, said, that an author's case was exactly similar to that of an inventor of a new mechanical machine; that both original inventions stood upon the same footing in point of property, whether the case were mechanical or literary, whether an epic poem or an orrery; that the immorality of pirating another man's invention was as great as that of purloining his ideas. Property in mechanical works or works of art, executed by a man for his own amusement, instruction, or use, is allowed to subsist, certainly, and may, before publication by him, be invaded, not merely by copying, but by description or by catalogue, as it appears to me. A catalogue of such works may in itself be valuable. It may also as effectually show the bent and turn of the

possessing no element of a literary nature is protected from piracy.[28]

---

mind, the feelings and taste of the artist, especially if not professional, as a list of his papers. The portfolio or the studio may declare as much as the writing-table. A man may employ himself in private in a manner very harmless, but which, disclosed to society, may destroy the comfort of his life, or even his success in it. Every one, however, has a right, I apprehend, to say that the produce of his private hours is not more liable to publication without his consent, because the publication must be creditable or advantageous to him, than it would be in opposite circumstances."

"I think, therefore, not only that the defendant here is unlawfully invading the plaintiff's rights, but also that the invasion is of such a kind and affects such property as to entitle the plaintiff to the preventive remedy of an injunction; and if not the more, yet, certainly, not the less, because it is an intrusion, — an unbecoming and unseemly intrusion, — an intrusion not alone in breach of conventional rules, but offensive to that inbred sense of propriety natural to every man, — if intrusion, indeed, fitly describes a sordid spying into the privacy of domestic life, — into the home (a word hitherto sacred among us), the home of a family whose life and conduct form an acknowledged title, though not their only unquestionable title, to the most marked respect in this country." Knight Bruce, V.C., in Prince Albert v. Strange, 2 DeGex & Sm. 652, 696, 697.

[28] Kiernan v. Manhattan Quotation Co., 50 How. Pr. 194 (1876).

That this protection cannot rest upon the right to literary or artistic property in any exact sense, appears the more clearly {203} when the subject-matter for which protection is invoked is not even in the form of intellectual property, but has the attributes of ordinary tangible property. Suppose a man has a collection of gems or curiosities which he keeps private: it would hardly be contended that any person could publish a catalogue of them, and yet the articles enumerated are certainly not intellectual property in the legal sense, any more than a collection of stoves or of chairs.[29]

---

[29] "The defendants' counsel say, that a man acquiring a knowledge of another's property without his consent is not by any rule or principle which a court of justice can apply (however secretly he may have kept or endeavored to keep it) forbidden without his consent to communicate and publish that knowledge to the world, to inform the world what the property is, or to describe it publicly, whether orally, or in print or writing.

"I claim however, leave to doubt whether, as to property of a private nature, which the owner, without infringing on the right of any other, may and does retain in a state of privacy, it is certain that a person who, without the owner's consent, express or implied, acquires a knowledge of it, can lawfully avail himself of the knowledge so acquired to publish without his consent a description of the property.

The belief that the idea of property in its narrow sense was the basis of the protection of unpublished manuscripts led an able court to refuse, in several cases, injunctions against the publication of private letters, on the ground that "letters not possessing the attributes of literary

"It is probably true that such a publication may be in a manner or relate to property of a kind rendering a question concerning the lawfulness of the act too slight to deserve attention. I can conceive cases, however, in which an act of the sort may be so circumstanced or relate to property such, that the matter may weightily affect the owner's interest or feelings, or both. For instance, the nature and intention of an unfinished work of an artist, prematurely made known to the world, may be painful and deeply prejudicial against him; nor would it be difficult to suggest other examples. . . .

"It was suggested that, to publish a catalogue of a collector's gems, coins, antiquities, or other such curiosities, for instance, without his consent, would be to make use of his property without his consent; and it is true, certainly, that a proceeding of that kind may not only as much embitter one collector's life as it would flatter another, — may be not only an ideal calamity, — but may do the owner damage in the most vulgar sense. Such catalogues, even when not descriptive, are often sought after, and sometimes obtain very substantial prices. These, therefore, and the like instances, are not necessarily examples merely of pain inflicted in point of sentiment or imagination; they may be that, and something else beside." Knight Bruce, V.C., in Prince Albert *v.* Strange, 2 DeGex & Sm. 652, 689, 690.

compositions are not property entitled to protection;" and that it was "evident the plaintiff could not have considered the letters as of any value whatever as literary productions, for a letter cannot be considered of value to the author which he never would consent to have published."[30]   But {204} these decisions have not been followed,[31] and it may not be considered settled that the protection afforded by the common law to the author of any writing is entirely independent of its pecuniary value, its intrinsic merits, or of any intention to publish the same and, of course, also, wholly independent of the material, if any, upon which, or the mode in which, the thought or sentiment was expressed.

---

[30] Hoyt *v.* Mackenzie, 3 Barb. Ch. 320, 324 (1848); Wetmore *v.* Scovell, 3 Edw. Ch. 515 (1842).   See Sir Thomas Plumer in 2 Ves. & B. 19 (1813).

[31] Woolsey *v.* Judd, 4 Duer, 379, 404 (1855).   "It has been decided, fortunately for the welfare of society, that the writer of letters, though written without any purpose of profit, or any idea of literary property, possesses such a right of property in them, that they cannot be published without his consent, unless the purpose of justice, civil or criminal, require the publication."   Sir Samuel Romilly, *arg.*, in Gee *v.* Pritchard, 2 Swanst. 402, 418 (1818).   But see High on Injunctions, 3d ed., § 1012, *contra.*

Although the courts have asserted that they rested their decisions on the narrow grounds of protection to property, yet there are recognitions of a more liberal doctrine. Thus in the case of Prince Albert *v.* Strange, already referred to, the opinions of both the Vice-Chancellor and of the Lord Chancellor, on appeal, show a more or less clearly defined perception of a principle broader than those which were mainly discussed, and on which they both place their chief reliance. Vice-Chancellor Knight Bruce referred to publishing of a man that he had "written to particular persons or on particular subjects" as an instance of possibly injurious disclosures as to private matters, that the courts would in a proper case prevent; yet it is difficult to perceive how, in such a case, any right of privacy, in the narrow sense, would be drawn in question, or why, if such a publication would be restrained when it threatened to expose the victim not merely to sarcasm, but to ruin, it should not equally be enjoined, if it threatened to embitter his life. To deprive a man of the potential profits to be realized by publishing a catalogue of his gems cannot *per se* be a wrong to him. The possibility of future profits is not a right of property which the law ordinarily recognizes; it must, therefore, be an infraction of other rights which constitutes the wrongful act, and that infraction is equally wrongful, whether its results are to forestall the profits that the individual himself might secure by giving the matter a publicity obnoxious to him, or to gain an advantage at the expense of his mental pain and suffering. If the fiction of property in a narrow sense must be preserved, it is still true that the end accomplished by the gossip-monger is attained by the use of that which {205} is another's, the facts relating to his private life, which he has seen fit to keep private. Lord Cottenham stated that a man "is that which is exclusively his," and cited with approval the opinion of Lord Eldon, as reported in a manuscript note of the case of Wyatt *v.* Wilson, in 1820, respecting an engraving of George the Third during his illness, to the effect that "if one of the late king's physicians had kept a diary of what he heard and saw, the court would not, in the king's lifetime, have permitted him to print and publish it;" and Lord Cottenham declared, in respect to the acts of the defendants in the case before him, that "privacy is the right invaded." But if privacy is once recognized as a right entitled to legal protection, the interposition of the courts cannot depend on the particular nature of the injuries resulting.

These considerations lead to the conclusion that the protection afforded to thoughts, sentiments, and emotions, expressed through the medium of writing or of the arts, so far as it consists in preventing publication, is merely an instance of the enforcement of the more general right of the individual to be let alone. It is like the right not be assaulted or beaten, the right not be imprisoned, the right not to be maliciously prosecuted, the right not to be defamed. In each of these rights, as indeed in all other rights recognized by the law, there inheres the quality of being owned or possessed — and (as that is the distinguishing attribute of property) there may some propriety in speaking of those rights as property. But, obviously, they bear little resemblance to what is ordinarily comprehended under that term. The principle which protects personal writings and all other personal productions, not against theft and physical appropriation, but against publication in any form, is in reality not the principle of private property, but that of an inviolate personality.[32] {206}

---

[32] "But a doubt has been suggested, whether mere private letters, not intended as literary compositions, are entitled to the protection of an injunction in the same manner as compositions of a literary character. This doubt has probably arisen from the habit of not

discriminating between the different rights of property which belong to an unpublished manuscript, and those which belong to a published book. The latter, as I have intimated in another connection, is a right to take the profits of publication. The former is a right to control the act of publication, and to decide whether there shall be any publication at all. It has been called a right of property; an expression perhaps not quite satisfactory, but on the other hand sufficiently descriptive of a right which, however incorporeal, involves many of the essential elements of property, and is at least positive and definite. This expression can leave us in no doubt as to the meaning of the learned judges who have used it, when they have applied it to cases of unpublished manuscripts. They obviously intended to use it in no other sense, than in contradistinction to the mere interests of feeling, and to describe a substantial right of legal interest." Curtis on Copyright, pp. 93, 94.

The resemblance of the right to prevent publication of an unpublished manuscript to the well-recognized rights of personal immunity is found in the treatment of it in connection with the rights of creditors. The right to prevent such publication and the right of action for its infringement, like the cause of action for an assault, battery, defamation, or malicious prosecution, are not assets available to creditors.

"There is no law which can compel an author to publish. No one can determine this essential matter of publication but the author. His manuscripts, however valuable, cannot, without his consent, be seized by his creditors as property." McLean, J., in Bartlett *v.* Crittenden, 5 McLean, 32, 37 (1849).

If we are correct in this conclusion, the existing law affords a principle from which may be invoked to protect the privacy of the individual from invasion either by the too enterprising press, the photographer, or the possessor of any other modern device for rewording or reproducing scenes or sounds. For the protection afforded is not confined by the authorities to those cases where any particular medium or form of expression has been adopted, not to products of the intellect. The same protection is afforded to emotions and sensations expressed in a musical composition or other work of art as to a literary composition; and words spoken, a pantomime

---

It has also been held that even where the sender's rights are not asserted, the receiver of a letter has not such property in it as passes to his executor or administrator as a salable asset. Eyre *v.* Higbee, 22 How. Pr. (N. Y.) 198 (1861).

"The very meaning of the word 'property' in its legal sense is 'that which is peculiar or proper to any person; that which belongs exclusively to one.' The first meaning of the word from which it is derived — *proprius* — is 'one's own.' " Drone on Copyright, p. 6.

It is clear that a thing must be capable of identification in order to be the subject of exclusive ownership. But when its identity can be determined so that individual ownership may be asserted, it matters not whether it be corporeal or incorporeal.

acted, a sonata performed, is no less entitled to protection than if each had been reduced to writing. The circumstance that a thought or emotion has been recorded in a permanent form renders its identification easier, and hence may be important from the point of view of evidence, but it has no significance as a matter of substantive right. If, then, the decisions indicate a general right to privacy for thoughts, emotions, and sensations, these should receive the same protection, whether expressed in writing, or in conduct, in conversation, in attitudes, or in facial expression.

It may be urged that a distinction should be taken between the {207} deliberate expression of thoughts and emotions in literary or artistic compositions and the casual and often involuntary expression given to them in the ordinary conduct of life. In other words, it may be contended that the protection afforded is granted to the conscious products of labor, perhaps as an encouragement to effort.[33] This

---

[33] "Such then being, as I believe, the nature and the foundation of the common law as to manuscripts independently of Parliamentary additions and subtractions, its operation cannot of necessity be confined to literary subjects. That would be to limit the rule by the example. Wherever the produce of labor is liable to invasion in an analogous manner, there must, I

contention, however plausible, has, in fact, little to recommend it. If the amount of labor involved be adopted as the test, we might well find that the effort to conduct one's self properly in business and in domestic relations had been far greater than that involved in painting a picture or writing a book; one would find that it was far easier to express lofty sentiments in a diary than in the conduct of a noble life. If the test of deliberateness of the act be adopted, much casual correspondence which is now accorded full protection would be excluded from the beneficent operation of existing rules. After the decisions denying the distinction attempted to be made between those literary productions which it was intended to publish and those which it was not, all considerations of the amount of labor involved, the degree of deliberation, the value of the product, and the intention of publishing must be abandoned, and no basis is discerned upon which the right to restrain publication and reproduction of such so-called literary and artistic works can be rested, except the right to privacy, as a part of the more general right to the immunity of the person, — the right to one's personality.

---

suppose, be a title to analogous protection or redress." Knight Bruce, V.C., in Prince Albert *v.* Strange, 2 DeGex & Sm. 652, 696.

---

It should be stated that, in some instances where protection has been afforded against wrongful publication, the jurisdiction has been asserted, not on the ground of property, or at least not wholly on that ground, but upon the ground of an alleged breach of an implied contract or of a trust or confidence.

Thus, in Abernethy *v.* Hutchinson, 3 L. J. Ch. 209 (1825), where the plaintiff, a distinguished surgeon, sought to restrain the publication in the "Lancet" of unpublished lectures which he had delivered as St. Batholomew's Hospital in London, Lord Eldon {208} doubted whether there could be property in lectures which had not been reduced to writing, but granted the injunction on the ground of breach of confidence, holding "that when persons were admitted as pupils or otherwise, to hear these lectures, although they were orally delivered, and although the parties might go to the extent, if they were able to do so, of putting down the whole by means of short-hand, yet they could do that only for the purposes of their own information, and could not publish, for profit, that which they had not obtained the right of selling."

In Prince Albert *v.* Strange, 1 McN. & G. 25 (1849), Lord Cottenham, on appeal, while recognizing a right of property in the etchings which of itself would justify the issuance of the injunction, stated, after discussing the evidence, that he was bound to assume that the possession of the etching by the defendant had "its foundation in a breach of trust, confidence, or contract," and that upon such ground also the plaintiff's title to the injunction was fully sustained.

In Tuck *v.* Priester, 19 Q. B. D. 639 (1887), the plaintiffs were owners of a picture, and employed the defendant to make a certain number of copies. He did so, and made also a number of other copies for himself, and offered them for sale in England at a lower price. Subsequently, the plaintiffs registered their copyright in the picture, and then brought suit for an injunction and damages. The Lords Justices differed as to the application of the copyright acts to the case, but held unanimously that independently of those acts, the plaintiffs were entitled to an injunction and damages for breach of contract.

In Pollard *v.* Photographic Co., 40 Ch. Div. 345 (1888), a photographer who had taken a lady's photograph under the ordinary circumstances was restrained from exhibiting it, and also from selling copies of it, on the ground that it was a breach of an implied term in the contract, and also that it was a breach of confidence. Mr. Justice North interjected in the argument of the plaintiff's counsel the inquiry: "Do you dispute that if the negative likeness were taken on the sly, the person who took it might exhibit copies?" and counsel for the plaintiff answered: "In that case there would be no trust or consideration to support a contract." Later, the defendant's counsel argued that "a person has no property in his own features; short of doing what is libellous or otherwise illegal, there is no restriction on the {209} photographer's using his negative." But the court, while expressly finding a breach of contract and of trust sufficient to justify its interposition, still seems to have felt the necessity of resting the decision also upon a right of property,[34] in order to

---

[34] "The question, therefore, is whether a photographer who has been employed by a customer to take his or her portrait is justified in striking off copies of such photograph for his own use, and selling and disposing of them, or publicly exhibiting them by way of advertisement or otherwise, without the authority of such customer, either express or implied. I say 'express or implied,' because a photographer is frequently allowed, on his own request, to take a photograph of a person under circumstances in which a subsequent sale by him must have been in the contemplation of both parties, though not actually mentioned. To the question

thus put, my answer is in the negative, that the photographer is not justified in so doing. Where a person obtains information in the course of a confidential employment, the law does not permit him to make any improper use of the information so obtained; and an injunction is granted, if necessary, to restrain such use; as, for instance, to restrain a clerk from disclosing his master's accounts, or an attorney from making known his client's affairs, learned in the course of such employment. Again, the law is clear that a breach of contract, whether express or implied, can be restrained by injunction. In my opinion the case of the photographer comes within the principles upon which both of these cases depend. The object for which he is employed and paid is to supply his customer with the required number of printed photographs of a given subject. For this purpose the negative is taken by the photographer on glass; and from this negative copies can be printed in much larger numbers than are generally required by the customer. The customer who sits for the negative thus puts the power of reproducing the object in the hands of the photographer; and in my opinion the photographer who uses the negative to produce other copies for his own use, without authority, is abusing the power confidently placed in his hands merely for the purpose of supplying the customer; and further, I hold that the bargain between the customer and the photographer includes, by implication, an agreement that the prints taken from the negative are to be appropriated to the use of the customer only." Referring to the opinions delivered in Tuck v. Priester, 19 Q. B. D. 639, the learned justice continued: "Then Lord Justice Lindley says: 'I will deal first with the injunction, which stands, or may stand, on a totally different footing from either the penalties or the damages. It appears to me that the relation between the plaintiffs and the defendant was such that, whether the plaintiffs had copyright or not, the defendant has done that which renders him liable to an injunction. He was employed by the plaintiffs to make a certain number of copies of the picture, and that employment carried with it the necessary implication that the defendant was not to make more copies for himself, or to sell the additional copies in this country in competition with his employer. Such conduct on his part is a gross breach of contract and a gross breach of faith, and, in my judgment, clearly entitles the plaintiffs to an injunction, whether they have a copyright in the picture or not.' That case is the more noticeable, as the contract was in writing; and yet it was held to be an implied condition that the defendant should not make any copies for himself. The phrase 'a gross breach of faith' used by Lord Justice Lindley in that case applies with equal force to the present, when a lady's feelings are shocked by finding that the photographer she has employed to take her likeness for her own use is publicly exhibiting and selling copies thereof." North, J., in Pollard v. Photographic Co., 40 Ch. D. 345, 349-352 (1888).

"It may be said also that the cases to which I have referred are all cases in which there was some right of property infringed, based upon the recognition by the law of protection being due for the products of a man's own skill or mental labor; whereas in the present case the person photographed has done nothing to merit such protection, which is meant to prevent legal wrongs, and not mere sentimental grievances. But a person whose photograph is taken by a photographer is not thus deserted by the law; for the Act of 25 and 26

36

Vict., c. 68, s. 1, provides that when the negative of any photograph is made or executed for or on behalf of another person for a good or valuable consideration, the person making or executing the same shall not retain the copyright thereof, unless it is expressly reserved to him by agreement in writing signed by the person for or on whose behalf the same is so made or executed; but the copyright shall belong to the person for or on whose behalf the same shall have been made or executed.

"The result is that in the present case the copyright in the photograph is in one of the plaintiffs. It is true, no doubt, that sect. 4 of the same act provides that no proprietor of copyright shall be entitled to the benefit of the act until registration, and no action shall be sustained in respect of anything done before registration; and it was, I presume, because the photograph of the female plaintiff has not been registered that this act was not referred to by counsel in the course of the argument. But, although the protection against the world in general conferred by the act cannot be enforced until after registration, this does not deprive the plaintiffs of their common-law right of action against the defendant for his breach of contract and breach of faith. This is quite clear from the cases of Morison v. Moat [9 Hare, 241] and Tuck v. Priester [19 Q. B. D. 629] already referred to, in which latter case the same act of Parliament was in question." Per North, J., ibid. p. 352.

This language suggests that the property right in photographs or portraits may be one created by statute, which would not exist in the absence of registration; but it is submitted that it must eventually be held here, as it has been in the similar cases, that the statute provision becomes applicable only when there is a publication,

{210} bring it within the line of those cases which were relied upon as precedents.[35]

This process of implying a term in a contract, or of implying a trust (particularly where a contract is written, and where these is no established usage or custom), is nothing more nor less than a judicial declaration that public morality, private justice, and general convenience demand the recognition of such a rule, and that the publication under similar circumstances would be considered an intolerable abuse. So long as these circumstances happen to present a contract upon which such a term can be engrafted by the judicial mind, or to supply relations upon which a trust or confidence can be erected, there may be no objection to working out the desired protection though the doctrines of contract or of trust. But the court can hardly stop there. The narrower doctrine may have satisfied the demands of society at a time when the abuse to be guarded against could rarely have arisen without violating a contract or a special {211} confidence; but now that modern devices afford

---

and that before the act of registering there is property in the thing upon which the statute is to operate.

[35] Duke of Queensberry *v.* Shebbeare, 2 Eden, 329; Murray *v.* Heath, 1 B. & Ad. 804; Tuck *v.* Priester, 19 Q. B. D. 629.

abundant opportunities for the perpetration of such wrongs without any participation by the injured party, the protection granted by the law must be placed upon a broader foundation. While, for instance, the state of the photographic art was such that one's picture could seldom be taken without his consciously "sitting" for the purpose, the law of contract or of trust might afford the prudent man sufficient safeguards against the improper circulation of his portrait; but since the latest advances in photographic art have rendered it possible to take pictures surreptitiously, the doctrines of contract and of trust are inadequate to support the required protection, and the law of tort must be resorted to. The right of property in its widest sense, including all possession, including all rights and privileges, and hence embracing the right to an inviolate personality, affords alone that broad basis upon which the protection which the individual demands can be rested.

Thus, the courts, in searching for some principle upon which the publication of private letters could be enjoined, naturally came upon the ideas of a breach of confidence, and of an implied contract; but it required little consideration to discern that this doctrine could not afford all the protection required, since it would not support the court in granting a remedy against a stranger; and so the theory of property in the contents of letters was adopted.[36] Indeed, it is difficult to conceive on what theory of the law the casual recipient of a letter, who proceeds to publish it, is guilty of a breach of contract, express or implied, or of any breach of trust, in the ordinary acceptation of that term. Suppose a letter has been addressed to him without his solicitation. He opens it, and reads. Surely, he has not made any contract; he has not accepted any trust. He cannot, by

---

[36] See Mr. Justice Story in Folsom *v.* Marsh, 2 Story, 100, 111 (1841): —

"If he [the recipient of a letter] attempt to publish such letter or letters on other occasions, not justifiable, a court of equity will prevent the publication by an injunction, as a breach of private confidence or contract, or of the rights of the author; and *a fortiori*, if he attempt to publish them for profit; for then it is not a mere breach of confidence or contract, but it is a violation of the exclusive copyright of the writer. ... The general property, and the general rights incident to property, belong to the writer, whether the letters are literary compositions, or familiar letters, or details of facts, or letters of business. The general property in the manuscripts remains in the writer and his representatives, as well as the general copyright. *A fortiori*, third persons, standing in no privity with either party, are not entitled to publish them, to subserve their own private purposes of interest, or curiosity, or passion."

opening and reading {212} the letter, have come under any obligation save what the law declares; and, however expressed, that obligation is simply to observe the legal right of the sender, whatever it may be, and whether it be called his right or property in the contents of the letter, or his right to privacy.[37]

A similar groping for the principle upon which a wrongful publication can be enjoined is found in the law of trade secrets. There, injunctions have generally been granted on the theory of a breach of contract, or of an abuse of confidence.[38] It would, of course, rarely happen

---

[37] "The receiver of a letter is not a bailee, nor does he stand in a character analogous to that of a bailee. There is no right to possession, present or future, in the writer. The only right to be enforced against the holder is a right to prevent publication, not to require the manuscript from the holder in order to a publication of himself." Per Hon. Joel Parker, quoted in Grigsby *v.* Breckenridge, 2 Bush. 480, 489 (1857).

[38] In Morison v. Moat, 9 Hare, 241, 255 (1951), a suit for an injunction to restrain the use of a secret medical compound, Sir George James Turner, V.C., said: "That the court has exercised jurisdiction in cases of this nature does not, I think, admit of any question. Different grounds have indeed been assigned for the exercise of that jurisdiction. In some cases it has been referred to property, in others to contract, and in others, again, it has been treated as founded upon trust

that any one would be in possession of a secret unless confidence had been reposed in him. But can it be supposed that the court would hesitate to grant relief against one who had obtained his knowledge by an ordinary trespass, — for instance, by wrongfully looking into a book in which the secret was recorded, or by eavesdropping? Indeed, in Yovatt *v.* Winyard, 1 J. & W. 394 (1820), where an injunction was granted against making any use or of communicating certain recipes for veterinary medicine, it appeared that the defendant while in the plaintiff's employ, had surreptitiously got access to his book of recipes, and copied them. Lord Eldon "granted the injunction, upon the ground of there having been a breach of trust and confidence;" but it would seem difficult to draw any sound legal distinction between such a case and one where a mere stranger

---

or confidence, — meaning, as I conceive, that the court fastens the obligation on the conscience of the party, and enforces it against him in the same manner as it enforces against a party to whom a benefit is given, the obligation of performing a promise on the faith of which the benefit has been conferred; but upon whatever grounds the jurisdiction is founded, the authorities leave no doubt as to the exercise of it."

wrongfully obtained access to the book.[39]
{213}

We must therefore conclude that the rights, so protected, whatever their exact nature, are not rights arising from contract or from special trust, but are rights as against the world; and, as above stated, the principle which has been applied to protect these rights is in reality not the principle of private property, unless that word be used in an extended and unusual sense. The principle which protects personal writings and any other productions of the intellect of or the emotions, is the right to privacy, and the law has no new principle to formulate when it extends this protection to the personal appearance, sayings, acts, and to personal relation, domestic or otherwise.[40]

---

[39] A similar growth of the law showing the development of contractual rights into rights of property is found in the law of goodwill. There are indications, as early as the Year Books, of traders endeavoring to secure to themselves by contract the advantages now designated by the term "goodwill," but it was not until 1743 that goodwill received legal recognition as property apart from the personal covenants of the traders. See Allan on Goodwill, pp. 2, 3.

[40] The application of an existing principle to a new state of facts is not judicial legislation. To call it such is to assert that the existing body of law consists practically

---

of the statutes and decided cases, and to deny that the principles (of which these cases are ordinarily said to be evidence) exist at all. It is not the application of an existing principle to new cases, but the introduction of a new principle, which is properly termed judicial legislation.

But even the fact that a certain decision would involve judicial legislation should not be taken against the property of making it. This power has been commonly exercised by our judges, when applying to a new subject principles of private justice, moral fitness, and public convenience. Indeed, the elasticity of our law, its adaptability to new conditions, the capacity for growth, which has enabled it to meet the wants of an ever changing society and to apply immediate relief for every recognized wrong, have been its greatest boast.

"I cannot understand how any person who has considered the subject can suppose that society could possibly have gone on if judges had not legislated, or that there is any danger whatever in allowing them that power which they have in fact exercised, to make up for the negligence or the incapacity of the avowed legislator. That part of the law of every country which was made by judges has been far better made that that part which consists of statutes enacted by the legislature." 1 Austin's Jurisprudence, p. 224.

The cases referred to above show that the common law has for a century and a half protected privacy in certain cases, and to grant the further protection now suggested would be merely another application of an existing rule.

44

exist, since already the value of mental suffering, caused by an act wrongful in itself, is recognized as a basis for compensation.

The right of one who has remained a private individual, to prevent his public portraiture, presents the simplest case for such extension; the right to protect one's self from pen portraiture, from a discussion by the press of one's private affairs, would be a more important and far-reaching one. If casual and unimportant state-{214}ments in a letter, if handiwork, however inartistic and valueless, if possessions of all sorts are protected not only against reproduction, but also against description and enumeration, how much more should the acts and sayings of a man in his social and domestic relations be guarded from ruthless publicity. If you may not reproduce a woman's face photographically without her consent, how much less should be tolerated the reproduction of her face, her form, and her actions, by graphic descriptions colored to suit a gross and depraved imagination.

The right to privacy, limited as such right must necessarily be, has already found expression in the law of France.[41]

---

[41] Loi Relative à la Presse. 11 Mai 1868.

It remains to consider what are the limitations of this right to privacy, and what remedies may be granted for the enforcement of the right. To determine in advance of experience the exact line at which the dignity and convenience of the individual must yield to the demands of the public welfare or of private justice would be a difficult task; but the more general rules are furnished by the legal analogies already developed in the law of slander and libel, and in the law of literary and artistic property.

1. The right to privacy does not prohibit any publication of matter which is of public or general interest.

In determining the scope of this rule, aid would be afforded by the analogy, in the law of

---

"11. Toute publication dans un écrit periodique relative à un fait de la vie privée constitue une contravention punie d'un amende de cinq cent francs.

"La poursuite ne pourra être exercée que sur la plainte de la partie interessée."

Riviére, Codes Francais et Lois Usuelles. App. Code Pen., p. 20.

libel and slander, of cases which deal with the qualified privilege of comment and criticism on matters of public and general interest.[42] There are of course difficulties in applying such a rule; but they are inherent in the subject-matter, and are certainly no greater than those which exist in many other branches of the law, — for instance, in that large class of cases in which the reasonableness or unreasonableness of an act is made the test of liability. The design of the law must be to protect those persons with whose affairs the community has no legitimate concern, from being dragged into an undesirable and undesired publicity and to protect all persons, whatsoever; their position or station, from having matters which they may {215} properly prefer to keep private, made public against their will. It is the unwarranted invasion of individual privacy which is reprehended, and to be, so far as possible, prevented. The distinction, however, noted in the above statement is obvious and fundamental. There are persons who may reasonably claim as a right, protection from the notoriety entailed by being made the victims of journalistic enterprise. There are others who,

---

[42] See Campbell *v.* Spottiswoode, 3 B. & S. 769, 776; Henwood *v.* Harrison, L. R. 7 C. P. 606; Gott *v.* Pulsifer, 122 Mass. 235.

in varying degrees, have renounced the right to live their lives screened from public observation. Matters which men of the first class may justly contend, concern themselves alone, may in those of the second be the subject of legitimate interest to their fellow-citizens. Peculiarities of manner and person, which in the ordinary individual should be free from comment, may acquire a public importance, if found in a candidate for public office. Some further discrimination is necessary, therefore, than to class facts or deeds as public or private according to a standard to be applied to the fact or deed *per se*. To publish of a modest and retiring individual that he suffers from an impediment in his speech or that he cannot spell correctly, is an unwarranted, if not an unexampled, infringement of his rights, while to state and comment on the same characteristics found in a would-be congressman could not be regarded as beyond the pale of propriety.

The general object in view is to protect the privacy of private life, and to whatever degree and in whatever connection a man's life has ceased to be private, before the publication under consideration has been made, to that extent the protection is likely to be withdrawn.[43]    Since, then, the propriety of publishing the very same facts may depend wholly upon the person concerning whom they are published, no fixed formula can be used to prohibit obnoxious publications. Any rule of liability adopted must have in it an elasticity which shall take account of the varying circumstances of each case, — a necessity which unfortunately renders such a doctrine not only more difficult of application, but also to {216} a certain extent uncertain in its operation and easily rendered abortive. Besides, it is only the more flagrant breaches of decency and propriety that could in practice be reached, and it is not perhaps desirable even to attempt to repress everything which the nicest taste and keenest sense of the respect due to private life would condemn.

---

[43] "Nos moeurs n'admettent pas la prétention d'enlever aux investigations de la publicité les actes qui relèvent de la vie publique, et ce dernier mot ne doit pas être restreint à la vie officielle ou à celle du fonctionnaire. Tout homme qui appelle sur lui l'attention ou les regards du publique, soit par une mission qu'il a reçue ou qu'il se donne, soit par le rôle qu'il s'attribue dans l'industrie, les arts, le théâtre, etc., ne peut plus invoquer contre la critique ou l'exposé de sa conduite d'autre protection que les lois qui repriment la diffamation et l'injure." Circ. Mins. Just., 4 Juin, 1868. Rivière Codes Français et Lois Usuelles, App. Code Pen. 20 n (b).

In general, then, the matters of which the publication should be repressed may be described as those which concern the private life, habits, acts, and relations of an individual, and have no legitimate connection with his fitness for a public office which he seeks or for which he is suggested, or for any public or quasi public position which he seeks or for which he is suggested, and have no legitimate relation to or bearing upon any act done by him in a public or quasi public capacity. The foregoing is not designed as a wholly accurate or exhaustive definition, since that which must ultimately in a vast number of cases become a question of individual judgment and opinion is incapable of such definition; but it is an attempt to indicate broadly the class of matters referred to. Some things all men alike are entitled to keep from popular curiosity, whether in public life or not, while others are only private because the persons concerned have not assumed a position which makes their doings legitimate matters of public investigation.[44]

---

[44] "Celui-la seul a droit au silence absolu qui n'a pas expressément ou indirectment provoqué ou authorisé l'attention, l'approbation ou le blâme." Corc. Mins. Just., 4 Juin, 1868. Rivière Codes Français et Lois Usuelles, App. Code Pen. 20 n (b).

2. The right to privacy does not prohibit the communication of any matter, though in its nature private, when the publication is made under circumstances which would render it a privileged communication according to the law of slander and libel.

Under this rule, the right to privacy is not invaded by any publication made in a court of justice, in legislative bodies, or the committees of those bodies; in municipal assemblies, or the committees of such assemblies, or practically by any communication in any other public body, municipal or parochial, or in any body quasi public, like the large voluntary associations formed {217} for almost every purpose of benevolence, business, or other general interest; and (at least in many jurisdictions) reports of any such proceedings would in some measure be accorded a like privilege.[45] Nor

---

The principle thus expressed evidently is designed to exclude the wholesale investigations into the past of prominent public men with which the American public is too familiar and also, unhappily, too well pleased; while not entitled to the "silence *absolu*" which less prominent men may claim as their due, they may still demand that all the details of private life in its most limited sense shall not be laid bare for inspection.

[45] Wason *v.* Walters, L. R. 4 Q . B. 73; Smith *v.* Higgins, 16 Gray, 251; Barrows *v.* Bell. 7 Gray, 331.

would the rule prohibit any publication made by one in the discharge of some public or private duty, whether legal or moral, or in conduct of one's own affairs, in matters where his own interest is concerned.[46]

---

[46] This limitation upon the right to prevent the publication of private letters was recognized early: — "But, consistently with this right [of the writer of letters], the persons to whom they are addressed may have, nay, must, by implication, possess, the right to publish any letter or letters addressed to them, upon such occasions, as require, or justify, the publication or public use of them; but this right is strictly limited to such occasions. Thus, a person may justifiably use and publish, in a suit at law or in equity, such letter or letters as are necessary and proper, to establish his right to maintain the suit, or defend the same. So, if he be aspersed or misrepresented by the writer, or accused of of improper conduct, in a public manner, he may publish such parts of such letter or letters, but no more, as may be necessary to vindicate his character and reputation, or free him from unjust obloquy and reproach." Story, J., in Folsom v. Marsh, 2 Story, 100, 110, 111 (1841).

The existence of any right in the recipient of letters to publish the same has been strenuously denied by Mr. Drone; but the reasoning upon which his denial rests does not seem satisfactory. Drone on Copyright, pp. 136-139.

3. The law would probably not grant any redress for the invasion of privacy by oral publication in the absence of special damage.

The same reasons exist for distinguishing between oral and written publications of private matters, as is afforded in the law of defamation by the restricted liability for slander as compared with the liability for libel.[47] The injury resulting from such oral communications would ordinarily be so trifling that the law might well, in the interest of free speech, disregard it altogether.[48] {218}

---

[47] Townshend on Slander and Libel, 4th ed., § 18; Odgers on Libel and Slander, 2d ed., p. 3.

[48] "But as long as gossip was oral, it spread, as regards any one individual, over a very small area, and was confined to the immediate circle of his acquaintances. It did not reach, or but barely reached, those who knew nothing of him. It did make his name, or his walk, or his conversation familiar to strangers. And what is more to the purpose, it spared him the pain and mortification of knowing that he was gossipped about. A man seldom heard of oral gossip about him which simply made him ridiculous, or trespassed on his lawful privacy, but made no positive attack upon his reputation. His peace and comfort were, therefore, but slightly affected by it." E.L. Godkin, "The Rights of the Citizen: To His Reputation." Scribner's Magazine, July, 1890, p. 66.

4. The right to privacy ceases upon the publication of the facts by the individual, or with his consent.

This is but another application of the rule which has become familiar in the law of literary and artistic property. The cases there decided establish also what should be deemed a publication, — the important principle in this connection being that a private communication of circulation for a restricted purpose is not a publication within the meaning of the law.[49]

5. The truth of the matter published does not afford a defence. Obviously this branch of the law should have no concern with the truth or falsehood of the matters published. It is not for injury to the individual's character that redress or prevention is sought, but for injury to the right of privacy. For the former, the law of slander and libel provides perhaps a sufficient safeguard. The latter implies the right not merely to prevent inaccurate portrayal of

---

Vice-Chancellor Knight Bruce suggested in Prince Albert v. Strange, 2 DeGex & Sm. 652, 694, that a distinction would be made as to the right to privacy of works of art between an oral and a written description or catalogue.

[49] See Drone on Copyright, pp. 121, 289, 290.

private life, but to prevent its being depicted at all.[50]

6. The absence of "malice" in the publisher does not afford a defence.

Personal ill-will is not an ingredient of the offence, any more than in an ordinary case of trespass to person or to property. Such malice is never necessary to be shown in an action for libel or slander at common law, except in rebuttal of some defence, *e.g.*, that the occasion rendered the communication privileged, or, under the statutes in this State and elsewhere, that the statement complained of was true. The invasion of the privacy that is to be protected is equally complete and equally injurious, whether the motives by which the speaker or writer was actuated are taken by themselves, culpable or not; just as the damage to character, and to some extent the tendency to provoke a breach of the peace, is equally the result of defamation

---

[50] Compare the French law.

"En prohibant l'envahissement de la vie privée, sans qu'il soit nécessaire d'établir l'intention criminelle, la loi a entendue interdire toute discussion de la part de la défense sur la vérité des faits. Le remède été pire que le mal, si un débat avait pu s'engager sur ce terrain." Circ. Mins. Just., 4 Juin, 1868. Rivière Code Français et Lois Usuelles, App. Code Penn. 20 n(a).

without regard to motives leading to its publication. Viewed as a wrong to the individual, this rule is the same pervading the whole law of torts, by which one is held responsible for his intentional acts, even though they care committed with no sinister intent; and viewed as a wrong {219} to society, it is the same principle adopted in a large category of statutory offences.

The remedies for an invasion of the right of privacy are also suggested by those administered in the law of defamation, and in the law of literary and artistic property, namely: —

1.  An action of tort for damages in all cases.[51] Even in the absence of special damages, substantial compensation could be allowed for injury to feelings as in the action of slander and libel.

2.  An injunction, in perhaps a very limited class of cases.[52]

It would doubtless be desirable that the privacy of the individual should receive the added protection of the criminal law, but for

---

[51] Comp. Drone on Copyright, p. 107.

[52] Comp. High on Injunctions, 3d ed., § 1015; Townshend on Libel and Slander, 4th ed., §§ 417a-417d.

this, legislation would be required.[53] Perhaps it would be deemed proper to bring the criminal

---

[53] The following draft of a bill has been prepared by William H. Dunbar, Esq., of the Boston bar, as a suggestion for possible legislation: —

"SECTION 1. Whoever publishes in any newspaper, journal, magazine, or other periodical publication any statement concerning the private life or affairs of another, after being requested in writing by such other person not to publish such statement or any statement concerning him, shall be punished by imprisonment in the State prison not exceeding five years, or by imprisonment in the jail not exceeding two years, or by fine not exceeding one thousand dollars; provided, that no statement concerning the conduct of any person in, or the qualifications of any person for, a public office or position which such person holds, has held, or is seeking to obtain, or for which such person is at the time of such publication a candidate, or for which he or she is then suggested as a candidate, and no statement of or concerning the acts of any person in his or her business, professional, or calling, and no statement concerning any person in relation to a position, profession, business, or calling, bringing such person prominently before the public, or in relation to the qualifications for such a position, business, profession, or calling of any person prominent or seeking prominence before the public, and no statement relating to any act done by any person in a public place, nor any other statement of matter which is of public and general interest, shall be deemed a statement concerning the private life or affairs of such person within the meaning of this act.

liability for such publication within narrower limits; but that the community has an interest in preventing such invasions of privacy, sufficiently strong to justify the introduction of such a remedy, cannot be doubted. Still, the protection of society must come mainly through a recognition of {220} the rights of the individual. Each man is responsible for his own acts and omissions only. If he condones what he reprobates, with a weapon at hand equal to his defence, he is responsible for the results. If he resists, public opinion will rally to his support. Has he then such a weapon? It is believed that the common law provides him with one, forged in the slow fire of the centuries, and to-day fitly tempered to his hand. The common law has always recognized a man's house as his castle, impregnable, often, even to his own officers engaged in the execution of its command. Shall the courts thus close the front entrance to constituted

---

"SECT. 2. It shall not be a defence to any criminal prosecution brought under section 1 of this act that the statement complained of is true, or that such statement was published without a malicious intention; but no person shall be liable to punishment for any statement published under such circumstances that if it were defamatory the publication thereof would be privileged."

authority, and open wide the back door to idle or prurient curiosity?

*Samuel D. Warren,*
*Louis D. Brandeis.*

BOSTON, December, 1890.

The most influential piece of legal scholarship in history, many scholars say, is this 1890 *Harvard Law Review* article by two young Boston lawyers (one of whom later became a legendary Supreme Court Justice). Warren and Brandeis created -- by cleverly weaving strands of precedent, policy, and logic -- the legal concept of privacy and the power of legal protection for that right. Their clear and effective prose stands the test of time, and influenced such modern notions as "inviolate personality," the law's "elasticity," and the problems of "piracy." They resisted the label of "judicial legislation" for their proposals. And they foresaw the threat of new technology.

Most of all, they asserted the fundamental "right to be let alone," and its implications to modern law are profound. Their privacy concept has grown into a constitutional law norm raising issues about abortion, drug testing, surveillance, sexual orientation, free speech, the "right to die," and medical confidentiality. All these spinoffs trace their origins to this master work. It is simply one of the most significant parts of the modern canon of law, politics, and sociology.

The new Foreword by Prof. Childress shares not only this import and effect, but also the fascinating backstory behind the article. Its origins are found in Warren's own prickly experiences with the press, famously after its reports on his family weddings. One myth was recently debunked: it could not have been his daughter's wedding that upset him. The newer legend is explained, including the role of *The Washington Post* and the emerging *paparazzi*. This was no mere academic exercise to Warren and Brandeis, it turns out.

The Foreword adds a biographical summary of each author, including some less-known questions about Brandeis's own judicial ethics later in life (debunking another myth), as well as discussing the possible tension between the privacy right and the First Amendment that Brandeis championed.

*Steven Alan Childress* is the Conrad Meyer III Professor of Law at Tulane University, where he teaches legal ethics, torts, and evidence. He earned his law degree from Harvard and a Ph.D. in Jurisprudence and Social Policy from Berkeley. He writes about federal courts, the First Amendment, and ethics. He co-authored *Federal Standards of Review*. Its 4th edition, published by LexisNexis in three volumes, is available in 2010; previous editions have been cited by over 300 courts, including the Supreme Court. He is a member of the California, D.C., and Supreme Court bars, Phi Beta Kappa, and the Law & Society Association.

For suggestions, questions, and inquiries, or to propose a new edition to the Legal Legends Series, please contact *quidprolaw@gmail.com*.

Made in the USA
Lexington, KY
18 April 2013